D0945224

In The
Grip
Of Prayer

Terry Magee

Intermedia Publishing Group

In The Grip Of Prayer

Published by:
Intermedia Publishing Group, Inc.
P.O. Box 2825
Peoria, Arizona 85380
www.intermediapub.com

ISBN 978-1-935529-36-1

Copyright © 2010 by Terry Magee
Printed in the United States of America
by Epic Print Solutions

DEDICATION

As this is my first book, there is a large list of people whom I wish to thank, who encouraged me in my journey and helped me reach this point. Even if they felt their contributions were small, I have appreciated their kindness and will thank them personally. In particular I wish to thank Terry Whalin and the team at Intermedia Publishing Group for guiding me through the process of getting a book to print.

I have had many mentors and encouragers in building my personal prayer life, including Joy Jacobs, Mark and Shirley Millward, and Marge Hobart. At the top of the list are Tom and Doris Roberts, certainly the strongest and most diligent prayer warriors I know. You have definitely led by example.

But most of all I wish to dedicate this book to my wonderful wife, Kim. You first taught me the passion to pray, and the desire to center everything around prayer. While I could have focused on an intellectual faith, you taught me the importance of simple, faithful prayer. God has blessed me greatly by bringing you into my life.

FOREWORD

Some call my wife, Alice, and I, "America's Prayer Coaches." True, we have written many books, taught conferences around the world, and have thousands in our free online school of prayer. But there are many "prayer coaches" in America and around the world. As matters have worsened around the world we see an increasing hunger in the hearts of believers to know God intimately and to know how to pray effectively. Christians want to see proof that they are being heard in heaven.

Like many things, most people assume it's more complicated than it really is. Those who know us well know that our heart is to demystify prayer and present it in its true biblical simplicity; not as a religious expression, but as a relational experience. Terry Magee knows that powerful effective prayer is based on a rich relationship with God and an understanding of His presence in us and His purposes for us.

Since our authority over darkness is no greater than our intimacy with Christ, we must spend time with Him. This is part discipline and part delight. Terry Magee's *In The Grip Of Prayer* is a practical instructional guide written to help us make a meaningful prayer connection. He teaches prayer as a life-style, rather than an event. With Terry's hand-based prayer pattern, you'll find the help you need to establish a life of continual, moment-by-moment prayer.

Whether you are a new Christian or a mature believer; whether you only have time for a quick prayer, or long to linger in His presence, Terry's book will guide you to a rich fellowship with the Lord. Prayer is the foundation of all that we do, May God bless you as you seek to deepen your intimacy with God and develop a life of prayer.

Eddie Smith, author, teacher and President, U.S. Prayer Center.

www.EddieAndAlice.com

INTRODUCTION

I was in Peru on a mission trip in the summer of 2006. We were working with a small church in one of the poor neighborhoods outside Lima, in an area where the residents literally carved their homes out of the steep hillsides. What had been rock and sand just a number of years ago was now a town, complete with homes, markets, schools, and churches. People moved to this town on the outskirts of Lima in search of a better life, and this church sought to bring them the eternal hope found in Jesus Christ. We were there that week to help this ministry, except that I was not feeling particularly helpful.

Spanish was their primary language, and I had struggled to learn even basic conversational words. My attempts to repeat the most basic phrases, while humorous to our gracious hosts, did not aid in communication. Although there was genuine caring and smiling at each other, without a translator I was reduced to gesturing and pointing.

I desired to minister to these Christians in

any way I could. I wished I could equip them in some way that would outlast my week there, and provide a means to help them as they sought to reach their community. Limited in my language skills, I could pray for them and with them, but was unable to teach anything to them.

As I considered ways to help teach them to pray, I thought of the ACTS (Adoration, Confession, Thanksgiving, Supplication) prayer acronym used to develop a balanced prayer life. I quickly realized that this prayer pattern, while useful in the United States, did not translate effectively into other languages. What could I do that would be helpful to those who spoke Spanish or any other non-English language?

One night while I was pondering this and praying for the people of this church and community, my mind went through the activities of the day. I thought of the children playing games and working on crafts, the adults digging into the hillside to carve space for a larger church, and the leaders playing instruments and cleaning the church. Then it hit me: in all these activities throughout the day people were using their *hands*. While different languages are spoken throughout the world and even within this church, all people have hands. How can our hands be a guide to remind us to pray, and to pray in a balanced and continual manner?

The ACTS acronym could be adapted to the human hand, shifting the English language acronym to individual fingers. Then we include the practice of surrender to God, which lifts the prayer pattern out of being a rote task to becoming more transformational. Our hands can guide us to a better prayer life through a continual reminder of interacting with God.

It is my desire that as you read this book this prayer pattern is not just added to your list of prayer tools, but is used to spend intimate time with God in prayer. My hope is that as you read this book and begin to practice this manner of praying, you are drawn closer to God in a simple yet powerful way. God desires that we love Him with all our heart, soul, mind, and strength. Using a physical part of us to engage spiritually with God helps bring our whole person into fellowship with God. My prayer for you is that you can use this prayer pattern to seek God with your whole person. Then you can know the joy of walking with God and abiding in God.

TABLE OF CONTENTS

TERRY MAGEE

Chapter 1

A HAND-Y GUIDE TO EFFECTIVE PRAYER

*D*eveloping an effective prayer life is like losing weight: despite how much I learn, I do not see much progress. In my quest to achieve a desired weight, I would read helpful books, learn proper habits, understand certain foods to avoid, memorize good eating patterns and methods, attend meetings to encourage good eating habits, and join clubs dedicated to attaining a proper weight and healthy lifestyle. Through the years I continued to learn more about how to reach a desired weight. However, after gaining all this knowledge concerning weight loss, I realized

I was not applying this knowledge with the consistency needed for long term change.

The same was true in my prayer life. I could read books on prayer, learn about habits to foster prayer, understand the attitudes to avoid which hampered prayer, memorize prayer patterns, attend prayer meetings, and even lead prayer ministries and attend prayer conferences. Even with all this added knowledge about prayer, I was not seeing the desired change toward a more effective prayer life. Just as the weight loss books were at home while reading a menu at a restaurant or passing an ice cream shop, the prayer books were at home while living the normal trials of life. Knowledge about the topic had not successfully translated into an improved lifestyle related to the topic. My knowledge had not become sufficiently personal to where it was part of me wherever I went. Discouragement from lack of progress ensued, followed by abandoning the latest method or pattern I tried to adopt.

Perhaps you have experienced similar struggles regarding prayer. (You may have had similar struggles with weight loss, but that is another topic for another book.) For many people, more time is spent learning about prayer and talking about prayer than actually praying. When faced with a tough situation, your impulse is to reason through solutions in your own mind rather than turning to God first. When you do turn to God, it more closely resembles reading a wish list to God rather than spending intimate time with the loving Father. This wish-list mentality deters rather than aids in building an ever closer relationship with God through moment-by-moment walking in fellowship. Efforts to make a permanent change do not stick, causing both discouragement and guilt. None of the truly good prayer methods and techniques learned have translated into a more effective prayer life.

The root of the problem appears to reside in the nature of human beings. We are spiritual beings, so we have a connection with God. But we are also physical beings, living in the physical world, and the majority of what we experience is due to some sort of physical stimulus. It takes practiced self-discipline to block out our physical surroundings in order to focus upon God, who is Spirit. While many people have used God's creation as a starting point for praise, we too often neglect the Creator to focus on the creation.

Despite this ongoing struggle, Christians truly desire fellowship with God, to live the life of daily walking with God, desiring the intimate spiritual bond even while living in the physical world. What if there was a means readily available to us in the physical world that, rather than distracting us from prayer, could instead prompt us to pray more? Even more, could this means prompt us to pray in a manner which focuses more on God rather than ourselves and our desires?

Take a close look at your hand. Hold it up in front of you and examine the back of your hand. Notice how your hand starts as one unit and then separates into the four fingers and thumb. Perhaps you have some calluses or scars that are a testimony of your work and activity throughout life, or even an injury sustained along your journey through life. The more closely you examine your hand, the more detail you can observe. Perhaps there are scratches and nicks, or wrinkles and spots. There are fingernails and cuticles, and the unique shape and design of our hands. There is amazing variety in our hands even though they follow a common design.

Now turn your hand over, and study your palm. Anything you wish to hold will rest in your palm. Obviously, the larger the item, the harder it will be to hold in your palm or be surrounded by your fingers. Move your fingers and thumb about, and notice how they seem to work in unison. When you move your fingers and thumb the lines formed from the natural bending of your hand are accentuated. The movement of one finger impacts movement in other fingers, and the thumb is naturally pulled toward the fingers to grip items more strongly. It is precisely the opposable thumb that provides the strength of our grip.

Our hands are an integral part of our bodies, critical to interacting with the physical world around us. We use them to reach out to our world and pull things in toward ourselves. In the same way, prayer is what we use to reach out to God and invite Him into relationship with ourselves. Prayer is our means of communication with God, of bringing the Lord of the Universe into intimate fellowship with our innermost being.

Just as we can closely examine our hands,

it is important to make a close examination of our prayer lives, as prayer is a barometer of our relationship with God. Is your prayer life healthy, or scarred and wounded? Is your prayer time working in unison with God, or out of joint and trying to impose your will upon God? Are you enjoying a variety of prayer types and styles, or has it deteriorated into bland sameness? Is your emphasis on God or yourself when you pray? These questions can help diagnose the relative healthiness and balance of your prayer life, including your attitude when praying. Do not be too discouraged if your prayer life seems sporadic or out of balance, God is always ready to work with you in building deeper fellowship.

Just as we use our hands to grip and hang on to things throughout each day, we can also use them as a reminder to spiritually reach out to God and build a balanced prayer life. The fingers on our hand can help spur us towards these types of prayer:

- Praise - the conscious act of acknowledging God for Who He is
- Confession - recognizing our own sinfulness in contrast to God's perfect Being

- Thanksgiving – responding with thankfulness towards what God has done for us
- Intercession – presenting the needs of others and ourselves before God
- Surrender – submitting our will to God's will and relying on God for all things

These five components of prayer can be balanced in daily times of enriched fellowship with God. In order to do this, begin with your hand opened wide and palm toward you, symbolic of opening your heart to God. Then, you can build a grip by starting with your pinky finger and closing each finger in turn as you complete each step of prayer.

Getting a Grip

We as Christians know that God is with us wherever we go through His Spirit dwelling within us. However, in our daily lives, we too often forget His presence and seek to make life work within our own strength. Our lives are spent either compartmentalized with special times set aside for God or in ongoing guilt knowing that we are not abiding in God in the way we could. Neither option is desirable, yet too much of our lives reside in those dreary, self-focused places. We need to get a better grip on living our life in step with God rather than specific appointments with God. We also need to shift the focus from ourselves to God, as we reach out to Him moment by moment and day by day.

We desire to be in constant fellowship with God and to deepen our relationship with God, but the daily crush of life becomes an impediment to the intimacy we desire. We set aside special times of closeness to grab what intimacy we can while longing for more. Yet God knows both the busyness of our lives and our desires to be in step with Him in a moment-by-moment relationship. Using part of us that is always physically present can help us move toward the ideal relationship with God. Our hands can become more than a tool attached to our bodies; they become a means by which we establish a stronger and more continual attachment to God.

From the beginning of our lives we train our hands to achieve different tasks. We start with basic functions such as feeding ourselves and writing, and advance to more complex tasks, such as cross-stitch or playing an instrument. A few people will engage in extremely sensitive tasks such as surgery or even defusing bombs. Whatever we do, we continue throughout our lives to engage our hands in both new and ongoing tasks.

As we use our hands throughout the day to perform needed tasks, we can also use our hands to remind us of the importance of connecting with God. Our hands can spur us on to build a more effective prayer life as a means of developing greater intimacy with God. Let us now examine each finger more closely to understand how our hands can prompt us to praying in a manner which will draw us closer to God.

Chapter 2

PRAISE:
WHAT APPEARS LITTLE IS ACTUALLY BIG

*T*he poor, overlooked little finger. Even the nickname "pinky" finger is derived from the Dutch word for little finger, 'pink.' It is usually the shortest finger on the hand, and takes the brunt of punishment dealt out to our hands. When we hold our hands out in a defensive position, it is the little finger on the front line, ready to stand guard for the hand and ultimately the body.

In spite of its diminutive stature, the little finger plays a key role in the functioning of the hand. It is also referred to as the anti-thumb, based upon its position opposite the thumb to help anchor the hand's grip. The position of the little finger on the hand serves notice that its importance looms larger than its size.

Likewise, praise can too often be ignored or diminished, seen as consuming time better spent in other prayer pursuits. Even confession often receives more focus than praise during prayer times, especially from those with repentant hearts. Often a lack of understanding about praise results in a lack of attention to praise. Therefore, a review of the nature of and basis for praise will help develop this crucial first part of a balanced prayer life.

Getting God's Attention

The Psalms are seen as a prayer book of the Israelites, and can also be used in that manner by Christians today. A cursory look at the Psalms will show that many of them opened with either a direct praise of God, or a call to praise God:

- "Ascribe to the LORD, O mighty ones, ascribe to the LORD

glory and strength. Ascribe to the LORD the glory due his name, worship the LORD in the splendor of his holiness." (Ps. 29:1-2, New International Version)

- "I will extol the LORD at all times; his praise will always be on my lips." (Ps. 34:1)
- "Great is the LORD, and most worthy of praise, in the city of our God, his holy mountain." (Ps. 48:1)
- "It is good to praise the LORD, and make music to your name, O Most High." (Ps. 92:1)
- "Praise the LORD, all you nations; extol him, all you peoples." (Ps. 117:1)
- "Praise the LORD. Praise the name of the LORD; Praise him, you servants of the LORD." (Ps. 135:1)

There is a specific reason that many of the Psalms begin with praise. To help understand this, take another look at your hand. Notice that when you close your hand to make a fist or a secure grip, the little finger seems to naturally lead the way. The other fingers follow right behind, but the little finger goes first. It is almost unnatural to close a grip beginning with the index finger; the little finger seems the natural and logical point opposite the thumb at which to start the grip.

In the same way, praise of God is the natural way to begin prayer. Ps. 100:4 encourages us to "enter his gates with thanksgiving, and his courts with praise." It makes sense, when beginning to speak with God, to acknowledge Him for his superior character and qualities. After all, why bother praying to someone who is not superior to us? So praise of God is the honest acknowledgement that He is superior to us. As Ps. 100:4 states about entering God's courts with praise, it is best to begin prayer with the practice of praise.

Beginning prayer times with praise is an effective means of getting God's attention as it sends the message that we are serious about our prayer time with Him. Remember that God already knows our hearts and attitudes before we even speak. Opening our prayers with praise is a reminder to ourselves that we are seeking God's help and comfort, and that He is a Being both able and worthy to accomplish what is needed in our lives. George Orwell said, "We have now sunk to a depth at which re-statement of the obvious is the first duty of intelligent men." While God's character qualities and attributes may seem obvious, it is a good practice to continually remind ourselves of these attributes.

One cautionary note about beginning prayers with praise: the pagans felt they needed to praise their gods in order to curry their favor and make their intercessions successful. This became a form of manipulation in which the priests and leaders used excessive praise of their gods as a means to get the god to do what the leaders wanted. The true God of the Bible does not need our praise to feel better about Himself, nor can He be manipulated into doing what we want through praise. The purpose of praise is for us to have the proper attitude about who God is, especially in relationship to ourselves.

Understanding God's Character

Praising God helps us to understand God's character, to know Who He is. Often this is through a declaration of His qualities, such as:

- His omnipotence, "The LORD reigns, let the earth be glad." (Ps. 97:1)
- His goodness, "For the LORD is good." (Ps. 100:5)
- His grace, "The LORD, the LORD, the compassionate and gracious God." (Ex. 34:6)
- His mercy, "Let us fall into the hands of the LORD, for his mercy is great." (2 Sam. 24:14)
- His omniscience, "Such knowledge is too wonderful for me, too lofty for me to attain." (Ps. 139:6,)

Notice that these are simple declarations of God's character. No case has been made for these attributes, nor is there any specific justification given that God deserves this description. The

Bible states these characteristics about God as self-evident facts. Moreover, in Ex. 34:6, God is declaring His compassion, love, and omnipotence about Himself. It is simply understood in the Bible that this is the description of God.

Obviously, if someone's behavior and decisions were in contradiction to statements made about them, either by themself or someone else, the statements would either drown in hypocrisy or become a source of mockery. Anyone continuing to make declarations that were patently false would quickly lose his credibility. Part of God's goodness is His integrity, where His actions do match His character, and we will see this constancy in Chapter 4 when we address thanksgiving. Bear in mind that the heart of praise is recognizing God's true character and declaring it. The proof or justification is not needed at this point; praise is simply acknowledging Who God is.

God's Name Defining His Nature

In the past, a person was frequently defined by their name. During the middle ages, the surname often reflected someone's trade, as in

"Fred the baker" becoming Fred Baker, or "Bob the miller" becoming Bob Miller. One of my favorite surnames is Hasemeier, adapted from the German for 'rabbit farmer.' Some names just conjure up interesting images of past relatives. Royalty often attached monikers describing that person, sometimes leaving little to the imagination. While too many kings and queens got the title "the great," Charles the Bald apparently had a hair loss problem, and Harald I the Lousy let his hair grow until having a severe head lice problem. For better or worse, names and nicknames defined the person.

Biblical names dealt less with external characteristics and looked more at the heart. Jacob's new name, Israel, reflected not only a physical wrestling with God but the ongoing struggle Jacob had in acknowledging God as Lord rather than taking matters into his own hands. Simon was renamed Peter by Jesus to reflect how his faith and confidence in Christ would be part of the solid foundation on which the church would be built following Christ's death and resurrection. The definition of biblical names reflected the person's character more than any physical attribute.

The numerous names of God in the Bible can be seen as reflecting His character qualities. Redeemer (Job 19:25); Rock, Fortress, and Deliverer (Ps. 18:2); the Mighty One (Ps. 50:1); Immanuel (Matt. 1:23); the Lamb of God (John 1:29); the Good Shepherd (John 10:11); and the Vine (John 15:5) are but a sampling of the names of God reflected in the Bible. Isa. 9:6 reminds us that He is "Wonderful Counselor, Mighty God, Everlasting Father, Prince of Peace." Studying these names of God within their Scriptural context gains a fuller understanding of God's nature and becomes a springboard from which to praise God.

The Israelite name for God was Yahweh, often rendered as Jehovah in modern times. Descriptors were attached to God's name in the Old Testament in order to reveal and teach His character qualities to the Israelites:

- Jehovah-Jireh (ji' ra) – Yahweh is Provider (Gen. 22:8, 14)
- Jehovah-Rapha (ra' fa) – Yahweh heals (Ex. 15:22-26)
- Jehovah-Nisse (nis' se) – Yahweh

is our banner – a sign of
deliverance and salvation (Ex.
17:10-16)

- Jehovah-Mekaddish (ma ka dish')
  – Yahweh who sanctifies – to be
  set apart, to be holy (Lev. 20:7, 8)
- Jehovah-Shalom (sha lom') –
  Yahweh is peace (Judg. 6:22-24)
- Jehovah-Tsidkenu (tsid ka' nu) –
  Yahweh our righteousness (Jer.
  23:5-6)
- Jehovah-Shammah (sham mah') –
  Yahweh is there (Ez. 48:35)
- Jehovah-Rohi (ro' e) – Yahweh is
  my shepherd (Ps. 23:1)

God has always desired to make Himself
known to mankind, to reveal His person and
character to us. The Bible records many names
of God, providing opportunities to know Him
better as He is revealed throughout its pages.
These names of God provide a good foundation
of knowledge about God from which to praise
Him in our prayer times.

Praise Tips

Since the human species is so consistently self-centered, it benefits our prayer lives to shift our focus from ourselves to God as quickly as possible. The little finger is well positioned to start our prayers with praise, as it is positioned on what is usually the outward side of our hand. The natural position of our hand, whether in defense, waving, or simple lifting it up places our little finger away from our body as compared to our thumb. This is a good reminder that prayer must start away from ourselves and focused on God. Praising God in our prayers is the right way to shift that focus, and beginning our prayer time with praise starts our prayer emphasis on God rather than on ourselves.

Although this tendency towards self-centeredness is known, breaking out of that pattern requires both diligence and some practical helps. First, wiggle your little finger as you get ready to pray. This may sound odd, but just as people would tie strings around their fingers as reminders (yet how this told them *what* they were supposed to remember was always a mystery), the mere association of your little finger with praising God can immediately shift your focus from what you want to Who God is. At this point all that is needed is the ways in which to praise God.

The names of God as listed above are always a good place to start. Rather than simply listing the names, build a full understanding of each name. Study the Bible passage associated with the name to learn the context. Most names are used in multiple places, so use a concordance (many Bibles have one in the back) to look up the references for a given name. With this deeper knowledge of the meaning of that name, you can praise God with fuller depth than merely repeating a word.

The Psalms are full of praises to God. Psalm 150 is a reminder to praise God at all times and in numerous ways. The Psalms that begin with praises listed in this chapter are also good examples. Many Psalms are laments, which will start out with either a specific grievance with God or a complaint directed at God. Yet many lament Psalms will conclude with an attitude of praise. Psalm 64, which begins with "Hear me, O God, as I voice my complaint" concludes with "Let the righteous rejoice in the LORD and take refuge in him; let all the upright in heart praise him." Often the Psalmists needed an attitude adjustment from God, and just reminding themselves of who God is gave them reason to rejoice even during their troubles. If you have been beaten up by life lately, perhaps a lament Psalm is a good place to shift your heart and attitude into praising God.

The little finger, the smallest digit on our hand and its first line of defense, is positioned away from our body. It sits there and can remind us that as we seek to encounter God through prayer, beginning with praise is the best means of switching our emphasis from ourselves to God. Praise helps us remember Who God is by declaring His character qualities and attributes. Our little finger plays a big role in helping us build a God-centered prayer life.

Chapter 3

CONFESSION:
THE LOGICAL SECOND STEP IN PRAYER

*7*he ring finger. The very name identifies its function, for the tradition in Western cultures has been to put wedding rings on this finger for both genders. So it could be said that this finger symbolizes the most intimate relationship on earth. Sadly, the commitment represented by the ring on this finger is too often broken or damaged, and just not taken seriously.

Notice how if you start with your hand open and begin to make a grip by closing your pinky finger, the ring finger naturally follows along?

This is how our hand is designed, and to hold your ring finger back while closing your pinky finger can be painful. The ring finger is designed to follow your pinky finger and join it in the palm of your hand as you close your fingers to make a grip.

In the same way, once we have spent time praising God, it should naturally occur to us that we do not share God's qualities of greatness and goodness. We are not all-knowing or all-powerful. In addition, we do not fully share the qualities that define God's goodness. Oh, we can be good in certain ways and times, but in our sinful nature we operate from mixed rather than pure motives. Selfishness and willfulness crop up in our lives like weeds, infecting us with an attitude of rebellion against God. We just want to do things our way and push God to the corner. We want God to be handy to grab on to in a crisis as a life preserver, but to not be in the center of our lives on an everyday basis. In short, we sin.

So we must address this sin in our lives. Although any one particular sin does not remove our salvation, sin can hamper our fellowship with God. Isa. 59:2 relates that God cannot hear our prayers due to the sin in our lives. A prayer time of confession is crucial to restoring our relationship with God. Keep in mind, confession is not a simple "I know I was wrong when I did this" prayer to get past the uncomfortable part and on to other prayers. This is a full process consisting of three steps: confession of sin, repentance toward God, and restoration with God.

Total Accountability before God

It seems as though accountability for actions is out of favor these days, but God apparently did not get the message. The characters in the Bible did not shirk their accountability for their actions either. David, in Psalm 51, pours out his heart before God after his sins of adultery and murder. He accepts full responsibility for his actions in Ps. 51:4, "Against you, you only, have I sinned; and done what is evil in your sight." First, notice that David states that his sin is against God, and only God. While the victims of his sins might object to this statement, David is stressing that all sin at its core is a rebellion against and rejection of God. Second, David states that what he has done is evil. There is no excusing his behavior or using a less harsh description of his actions. David was totally honest with God and accountable for what he had done.

The prayers in the Bible emphasized confession of sin as a precursor to further prayer with God. Most of Daniel's prayer in Daniel 9 is spent in confession: "O Lord, we and our kings, our princes and our fathers are covered with shame because we have sinned against you." He is carrying an attitude of shame due to his sin against God. Many of the sins Daniel is confessing were not his own but occurred either before he was born, was very young, or was already removed from Jerusalem. Daniel is taking the sins of his people on his shoulders. When there is trouble, we don't want to take responsibility for our own actions, much less anyone else's actions. But Daniel stands up and accepts responsibility for his people's rebellion against God.

These prayers of confession, although recorded in Scripture, were private in nature. While there are examples of public prayers of confession in the Bible, such as in Nehemiah 9, confession to God was generally between that individual and God. So there is no need to hang out a laundry list of sins in public for all to see. The important part of confessing our sin is total honesty and accountability before God, which is best done in a private time of prayer with God. Reconciliation with others can occur later; this is the time to throw ourselves at the feet of God and acknowledge our sin against Him, pleading for His mercy on us.

Turning Away from Sin and Toward God

All the best-intentioned confession of sin will accomplish nothing if there is no change of heart. If there is no heart change, we are stuck in a sin-confession-sin cycle. If we remain in this cycle long enough, it is reasonable to question how serious we are about dealing with the sin in our lives. This is not meant to condemn those who wrestle with a chronic or habitual sin and are struggling to escape its bondage. But we do need to allow God to transform our hearts.

This concept of turning away from sinful attitudes is called repentance. David pleads for this in Ps. 51:10 when he asks for God to "Create in me a clean heart." David knows his only path away from sinfulness is for God to transform his heart. It does nothing for our relationship with God to simply confess our sins; we must also renounce the attitude and heart condition responsible for sinfulness.

So we must examine our hearts. Are we truly sorry for what we have done? Do we truly desire God to not merely forgive us but to transform us? Because of our sinful nature, we will have a bent toward sin. In the case of habitual or chronic sins, we will be shackled by bonds too strong to escape by means of our own strength. It is only by turning our hearts over to God that He can transform us to no longer desire what was previously pursued. We must change our direction and set ourselves in a new path by turning away from sin and toward God. This is when God knows we are serious about dealing with the sin in our lives. This is when a simple prayer of confession becomes a desire to start a new life with God.

Restoration of Fellowship with God

Once we have confessed and renounced our

sins, we are ready to restore our relationship with God. David says it best in Ps. 51:12, "Restore to me the joy of my salvation." Notice that David was not concerned with losing his salvation. But he had lost the joy of his relationship with God. He knew, as Isaiah knew, that his sin had separated him from God. Daniel and others from the time of the exile also knew that God was just in his judgments and they deserved what they got. In all these cases, the prayer of confession is followed by a plea for restoration.

God is a loving God. He has always desired fellowship with man; it is man who has turned his back on God. The story of the Prodigal Son is a beautiful picture of how a loving God runs to meet the sinful child who has learned the error of his ways and is ready to return in submission to his father. We must never doubt that when we are ready to renounce our sinfulness, God is more than ready to embrace us in fellowship.

But we must be ready to accept God's forgiveness. Too often, we continue to flog ourselves over past sins, especially the repeat offenses. Do we not believe that Christ's death on the cross paid the penalty for our sins? Have we not accepted God's gift of grace offered freely to us? If we have accepted God's gift of grace, why do we continue to punish ourselves when God has already completed the work? This is faithlessness, and it will continue to damage our relationship with God.

Grace is hard to accept. We know we don't deserve God's favor and blessing, but that is the very definition of grace. We want to somehow either earn our salvation, which is both wrong and impossible, or more insidiously, try to pay God back for what He has done for us, which is equally wrong and impossible. In the parable of the unmerciful servant (Matt. 18:23-35), he had an impossible sum to repay but was released from his debt by his master. We have been released from a similarly unpayable debt of sin by God through Christ. We must never try to pay it back or earn a portion of it; we must simply accept God's wonderful gift of forgiveness and grace.

A Note on Unforgiveness

Equally damaging to our fellowship with God is an attitude of unforgiveness. To continue the parable of the unmerciful servant, the same servant who had just been released from an impossible debt refused to show mercy to a fellow servant who had a minor debt. We have all suffered injustice from others or even been collateral damage of the sins of others. This damage has generally been minor, occasionally major, and in some occasions even traumatic. But the greatest of our injustices pales in comparison with our lifetime of sinfulness against God.

So, hard as it is, we must, as Jesus prayed in Matt. 6:12, "forgive our debtors." Both here and in the parable of the unmerciful servant, God's forgiveness of us is tied to our forgiveness of others. Make no mistake: God's forgiveness is not conditional upon our forgiveness of others, and neither is His forgiveness earned through forgiving others. The point of the parable is that the overwhelming grace extended to us from God for an unpayable debt must be extended to those around us who incur infinitesimally smaller debts. In the parable of the unmerciful servant, both men were repentant, and that is the point where grace is freely extended. As the unmerciful servant showed, his repentance was only temporary. A failure to extend grace to others is usually a sign of deeper spiritual issues.

Therefore, let us not cling to wrongs done to us by others, simmering in unforgiveness until we reap a harvest of bitterness. Let us rather keep short accounts with others in our community, quick to both ask for forgiveness and extend forgiveness. As Paul says in Rom. 13:8, "Let no debt remain outstanding, except the debt to love one another."

While this section focused on our acts of person-to-person forgiveness, this principle applies with God as well. Do not delay to seek God's forgiveness, and do not hesitate to receive God's forgiveness. Keeping short accounts will help us in maintaining close fellowship with God as well as overall spiritual health.

Not a Step with which to Take Shortcuts

Admitting our shortcomings is always uncomfortable, and many people do not take criticism well, resorting to defensiveness and retaliation. It is never pleasant and usually painful to have our faults placed before us. This pain intensifies if we come to the realization that our sin is actually a manifestation of a deeper character flaw, that it is part of what defines us. We cannot just say, "I did so and so…" but have to admit that "I am a …" Both the realization of sin and the larger realization of a character flaw can cut deep wounds into our egos.

It is precisely because of this discomfort and ongoing wounding of our pride that we try to hasten this forgiveness process. We want the pain to go away, so we stop the confession. We rationalize that since the process of confession is painful, stopping the confession will stop the pain. This is unwise, because sin not fully dealt with will always resurface later.

Many years ago, I had a tumor surgically removed. As I was recovering in the hospital, I thanked the visiting surgeon for his surgical group's act of healing. The wise surgeon replied, "Oh, we surgeons do not heal anyone. We just take out what is bad and then your body heals itself."

In the same way, confession is like spiritual surgery. The full process of confession, consisting of confession of sin, repentance toward God, and restoration with God, removes what is bad in our hearts and souls. Then we are free to continue in the lifetime healing journey in fellowship with God.

So do not hurry through this step. Let your ring finger be an ever present reminder of your commitment to God through Christ. Take the time needed to bare yourself before God, being totally honest and accountable to God, and let Him work to cleanse you from your sin. Then accept, truly accept, God's amazing gift of grace and go forward in your life in wonderful fellowship with Him. For confession is not the end of our prayer time, but merely a cleansing in preparation for the next step.

Chapter 4

THANKSGIVING:
RESPONSE TO GOD'S WORK IN OUR LIVES

*T*he illustrious middle finger stands taller than his comrades, anchoring the middle of the hand. Most everything you grip will be touched by your middle finger. It is this feature of the middle finger that provides the basis for some very crucial deception.

In baseball, the middle finger is the key to gripping the ball and delivering different pitches. The pitcher can push his middle finger to one side or the other to produce different spins, causing the ball to curve in different ways. But the real deception comes with the change of pace pitch, or change-up, as it is commonly known. The pitcher will throw the ball so that it has the same spin as a fastball. The batter, having less than half a second to recognize the pitch, will see the spin of a fastball and begin his swing, not wanting to be too late. However, the change-up is only about seventy-five percent as fast as a fastball, so the batter is ahead of the pitch and either hits the ball poorly or misses altogether. Greg Maddux, one of the greatest pitchers of modern times, had an unimpressive fastball compared to other pitchers but built his success on his extremely deceptive change-up. The source of the change-up's deceptively slow speed? The middle finger is not on the ball. A pitcher gets his power from his middle finger, so all successful change-ups are achieved by keeping the middle finger off the baseball, thus reducing the power behind the pitch and the speed of the ball.

We can deceive ourselves as well, and feel that all is well in our worlds. When we are sailing through life problem-free we can too easily take credit for our success. When we make it through trials, we can attribute the victory to our efforts.

The Israelites were warned of this tendency to forget God in Deut. 6:10-12. Once they had reached the Promised Land, with its nice cities and houses, fields and wells, and plenty to eat, they would be tempted to "forget the Lord, who brought you out of Egypt, out of the land of slavery."

It is easy to be dependent on God when things are tough, but our ongoing temptation is to believe that we are self-reliant when times are prosperous. When we forget God and His ongoing work in our lives we deceive ourselves. Everything looks fine, but the deception is that we are responsible for our prosperity and no longer need God. Our middle finger can remind us that we must always have an attitude of thanksgiving towards God. This is not meant to encourage fatalism and wait on God for all things, but to properly credit God for the good things in our lives.

The Distinction between Praise and Thanksgiving

We must always thank God for what He has

done in our lives. After a time of praising God and acknowledging our sin before God, it should be natural to thank God. After all, it is by His grace that we are restored into fellowship with Him. God's blessings can continue to flow even while our lives are flawed by sin. We must always remember what God has done in our lives.

It is easy to blur praise and thanksgiving together, because they are similar in nature. Both praise and thanksgiving are focused on God and are emphasizing God's character qualities. However, the distinction between the two is that praise is acknowledging Who God is, while thanksgiving is focusing on what God has done. Praise emphasizes Person and character while thanksgiving emphasizes actions and deeds.

While we may blend prayers of praise and thanksgiving together in our prayer time, it helps to have a clear understanding of the relationship between them. God's character will prompt His activities. Because God is love, He will always act from a place of love. Because God is a provider, He will be the source of all things. Because God is the Wonderful Counselor, He is the source of Godly counsel and wisdom. In summary, God does what He is; there is no inconsistency or hypocrisy with God. God's actions flow out of His character.

Remembering God's Track Record

The Bible presents a wonderful history of God fulfilling His promises to provide for His people. In fact, it can be said that the essence of history as recorded in the Bible is God redeeming man and drawing mankind back to Himself. There are countless examples of what God has done as part of this act of redemption. The Old Testament recounts a major example in God delivering the nation of Israel from bondage in Egypt. Psalm 136 lists God's wonderful acts for His people, beginning with creation and continuing through God delivering the people from Egypt.

We should examine our own lives as well, beginning with the time prior to our salvation, and see how God was working in and around us to draw us to Him. Then after that initial event, we should be able to recognize examples of God working in our lives each day. Some acts may be very significant while other events will be subtle and easy to miss. While we cannot always recognize God's subtle hand in the present, we should be able to look back through our lives and see specific things God has done for us.

Another whole category of thanksgiving is based on God's acts of general grace. Examples of this grace are His bringing rain and sun in their seasons to provide plenty to eat, and His design of creation to naturally supply our needs. These can be hard to recognize, but can be easily seen when we look, such as the cool shade of a large tree on a hot day, the unabashed affection of a favorite pet, the car starting and running well when in a hurry. These things can all be seen as simply the world working as it should, or we can understand God's handprint in all of creation when He proclaimed it as good.

The Author of all Good Things

Part of maintaining an attitude of thanksgiving is recognizing that God is the giver of all good gifts, as proclaimed in James 1:17. Our temptation is to be so busy in our days that we gloss over the small things in our lives. Sometimes

God uses major events or crises to make us stop and look more closely at our world. Before we reach that point, we need to look at the little or even micro blessings that occur throughout the day.

While the Bible often focuses on the spiritual gifts, it also presents examples of material blessings or simply good health and peace. Therefore we need to focus on both types of blessings in our lives. God's goodness provides numerous examples of physical blessings in our lives, from daily health to go about our days, to something as small as the sun shining when moving furniture and possessions that need to stay dry. In the spiritual realm, God's blessings do not stop with salvation. God sends friends at the right time with a note or phone call, providing the right level of support. God is patient with us when we fail, gently bringing us back into fellowship with Him. God is blessing us in numerous ways; it is up to us to stop and take notice.

Therefore, the key factor in maintaining an attitude of thanksgiving is to adjust the way we perceive events. We need to acknowledge God as the author of all good things both large and small. We need to recognize and be thankful for God's continual hand in our lives. Then we start to see events as blessings from God and not just random events happening to us. This is the path to building a thankful heart; to know God as the giver of all good gifts.

Our Source of Hope

The Old Testament writers always looked to God as their source of hope. Even when their circumstances were bad, they continually looked to God. Psalm 69, known as a lament Psalm, begins with a plea to God for help. The Psalmist describes his plight in detail while proclaiming his faithfulness to God. By the end of the Psalm, he is praising and thanking God for what he expects God to do. Because his hope is in God, and he knows the character of God, he thanks God in advance for the good things God will do in his life.

The Psalmist takes thanksgiving to a new level. Rather than waiting for God to act before expressing thanksgiving, his attitude is one of thankfulness even as he prays for deliverance.

Part of an attitude of thanksgiving is believing that God will act in a manner which will merit our thanksgiving. This thanking God in advance becomes a combination of thanksgiving and faith as we place our hope in God. Do we have the faith to expect that God will act in our lives in a manner consistent with His character?

Blending Praise and Thanksgiving

While praise and thanksgiving are being examined separately for emphasis, it is easy and natural to blend them together in a prayer time. As mentioned above, since God does what He is, we can take the names of God as a basis for seeing what God has done in our lives. Do not worry about blending praise and thanksgiving, but be aware of the distinct role played by each in our prayer lives.

The Psalmists regularly blended praise and thanksgiving. Psalms 90-110 are a good source of both praise and thanksgiving. They will call the people to sing and worship before God, and they will list His deeds that have initiated the worship. If you find yourself not feeling particularly thankful, or not recalling God's acts in your life for which to be thankful, read through these Psalms. Take God's deeds and character described and apply it to your own life. The themes of salvation, protection, and provision should prompt personal examples for which to be thankful.

Another thankfulness exercise is recognizing a monument to God's work in your life. When the Israelites crossed the Jordan River to enter the Promised Land, God had them take twelve stones from the river to their campsite. These stones were to be a memorial to the people of Israel so they would remember how God delivered them from bondage in Egypt and brought them safely into the Promised Land. While we do not build memorials out of stones as often today, you should be able to identify physical things around you that are memorials to God's ongoing work in your life. Then you can use that memorial as a springboard to thanking God.

Just as your middle finger is in the center of your hand, it can remind you that God is constantly in the center of your life, working on your behalf. Even during times of trial or attack, when you feel as surrounded and besieged as the

Israelites, you can place your hope in God. Just like the Israelites, you can thank God in advance for the great work He is going to do in your life.

Take a look at the first three fingers of your hand – the pinky finger, ring finger, and middle finger. See how they appear to work as a unit. They fit easily together in your hand as you build a grip. This is a reminder of how easily praise, confession, and thanksgiving work together in prayer to draw us into God's presence. We should feel humbled and thankful, overjoyed to be in the presence of God. At this point in our prayer time, we have allowed God to work in our hearts and turn our attitude toward Him and His work in our lives. Now we are ready to move to our next step in prayer, building our grip on our prayer lives.

Chapter 5

INTERCESSION: OUR REQUESTS BEFORE GOD

*T*he index finger sits in a very strategic position on our hands. It is the closest finger to the thumb, and can easily work with the thumb like a set of tongs. It is also used by itself to extract objects from our eyes, write in the sand or dirt, and is often the first finger used in any detail work, including finger painting. Of all our fingers, the index finger seems to be the one that can operate by itself, and therein lies the temptation.

Our index finger is used to represent intercessory prayer, or making requests to God, and it can become too easy to center our prayer life in the area of asking God for things. We want either material items or answers, and can focus our relationship with God on seeking all the wonderful things He can provide for us. But our relationship and prayer time with God must not be too consumed in taking what we can from God. We must balance our relationship with God, so we must return to the truth that our index finger, however independently it may be able to function, is a member of the working team that is our hand.

Our index finger also is normally the finger with which we point, so it is used to call attention to someone or something. Part of pointing can be to provide a direction by indicating with our finger. In the same way, our index finger can remind us of that time in prayer where we call God's attention to our concerns. Because the index finger is used to guide in the proper direction, we can be reminded to look to God to allow this part of our prayer time to be guided by Him.

Putting Intercession in its Place

Just as our index finger is fourth in line when starting at the pinky finger and moving towards the thumb, its position can remind us to place intercessory prayer in line after we have completed praise, confession, and thanksgiving. At the point in our prayer time when we are ready to present our requests to God, our attitudes and hearts should be more where God wants us to be. In fact, we may alter or even drop some requests as being out of line with God's will. Or we may have softened our hearts regarding a conflict with someone. Either way, the time spent in prayer prior to our intercession will influence the nature and direction of our intercession.

Obviously, there may be a crisis in which we do not have time to work through a period of praise, confession, and thanksgiving prior to making a request of God. In Matthew 14, Jesus walked on the lake toward the disciples and Peter got out of the boat to meet Jesus. When Peter began to sink, he did not work through other types of prayer, but called out, "Lord, save me!" God understands our instant calling on Him in an emergency; in fact He desires and welcomes our dependence on Him. In a moment of urgency, we must address the source of the crisis. However, in non-crisis times, intercession should be deferred until after we have spent time getting our hearts aligned with God.

Proper Petitioning of God

While there is no proper formula in bringing our requests before God, it is helpful to understand the different ways in which we can reach out to God with our concerns. The term 'intercessory prayer' is often used as an umbrella to describe any type of making requests of or expressing needs to God. These following definitions are designed to provide a fuller understanding of request-based prayer. They do not have to work in any order, they simply represent different types of requests we can make before God.

The first type of request is intercessory prayer. As mentioned above, this term can represent the whole range of requests, but it is used here to describe a specific type of request. To intercede means to go before one party on behalf of a third party. This is done all the time in our daily lives, for example, when parents go to a school teacher on behalf of their child. The person doing the interceding is appealing to someone in a position of higher authority in hopes of obtaining a favorable result for the person they represent. In intercessory prayer, we are taking the needs of other people and presenting them to God. The person for whom we are interceding may or may not be able to beseech God themselves. We are making additional requests to God on their behalf. A good example of an intercessory prayer is John 17:6-26, where Jesus prays for his disciples and all believers.

The second type is supplication prayer. To supplicate means "to ask for humbly" or "to beseech." The humility shown by a supplicant shows that they see themselves as lower than the person to whom they make their entreaty. The supplicant's hope is that the person in higher authority has the power and good will to grant what they desire. The key distinction between intercession and supplication is that an intercessor is going on behalf of someone else, while a supplicant is going on behalf of himself. The supplicant may not be by himself, but he will be part of the group he represents. Supplication prayer is personal, where we go before God with our requests. A good example of a supplication prayer is John 17:1-5, where Jesus prays for himself during the Last Supper. Peter's prayer to be saved from sinking in the Matthew 14 account mentioned above is also an example of supplication.

Petitions can be either intercessions or supplications, but they are more formal in nature. They are often part of a solemn occasion, and their form is often more liturgical than conversational. Solomon's prayer in 1 Kings 8 during the Temple dedication is a good example of a petition, as it is part of a formal ceremony.

It is not important to segregate these types of prayers, but to understand their roles, particularly the distinction between intercession and supplication. We must constantly guard ourselves against being self-focused. Christ's prayer in John 17 devoted the bulk of the time to others. He did not neglect himself, but placed his emphasis on others' needs. One feature to all types of request-based prayer is an acknowledgement that God is greater than us. After all, why waste our time seeking the help of someone lesser than us? If we did not have someone higher than us to whom we could seek help, we would just take matters into our own hands. The very fact that we are seeking God's help is an acknowledgement that He is more powerful than us. We have already expressed this in our praise time, but delivering our requests to Him is but a reinforcement of that truth.

Natural, but not Too Natural

Because our temptation to be self-centered is as likely to occur as water flowing downhill rather than uphill, it can be too easy to pray for ourselves. However, assuming we have gone through the effort of letting God work on our heart prior to presenting our requests before Him, this type of prayer should come quite naturally to us. We know what we need or want, and we are often made aware of what others need. The task, then, is to simply present these needs and wants before God.

'Simply' is a good motto to follow in

intercessory prayer. Jesus warned people against praying with many words or babbling on endlessly. He then taught what is known as The Lord's Prayer, presenting supplication in a simple and straightforward manner. Once we have worked through praise, confession, and thanksgiving, our hearts and souls should be aligned with God. Therefore, we do not need to take the time to make the case for why our specific request should be satisfied. God already understands and knows the need, we must simply state it.

We do not need training to know how to ask for things, as we started that as soon as we learned that asking would get us something we wanted. The key is to not fall into a selfish trap of emphasizing this type of prayer. We also do not want to be the sole source of our requests, but to have God as the author of our petitions rather than our own natures. A good example of letting God author our petitions, or at least the details, is in Neh. 1:10, where Nehemiah prayed to God to "give your servant success today by granting him favor in the presence of this man." Nehemiah knew what he wanted; he wanted success. However, he allowed God to be the author of precisely what form that success would take.

When we do not Know What to Pray

One big issue with making requests is that we might not know for what we are to pray. There are times when it will be very obvious, as it was to Peter in Matthew 14 as he was sinking into the water. Other times we will be like Nehemiah, where we have a general idea of what is wanted but really do not know the details, so we leave them to God. Yet still other times we simply do not know how to pray. We have our feelings and desires, but may be too emotionally caught up in the situation to be seeking God. Or we might see multiple options and do not know how to pray.

Paul provides the answer in Rom. 8:26-27; "In the same way, the Spirit helps us in our weakness. We do not know what we ought to pray for, but the Spirit himself intercedes for us with groans that words cannot express. And he who searches our hearts knows the mind of the Spirit, because the Spirit intercedes for the saints in accordance with God's will."

When we do not know what to pray for,

we lift that up to God. Remember, the most important part of prayer is aligning our hearts and souls with God. So in those times where we desire God's will yet do not clearly see it, we lay that uncertainty as a request before God, because the Holy Spirit will intercede on behalf of us in accordance with God's will. Sometimes God only gives us enough light for the next step, and we have to take each step with faith. When we do not understand the right request to make, we hand our request over to God through the Holy Spirit and let the Spirit intercede for us.

God has given us the Bible to see His working with mankind throughout history. How can we believe and trust that God will indeed do what He says? As Patrick Henry said, "I can only understand the future by knowing the past." God has given us, both in His written Word and in past experiences of our lives, a record of fulfilling His promises. Therefore, in those times when we do not know what to pray, we can place our requests in the hands of a trustworthy God.

God and Other-Focused

At risk of beating this point senseless, request-based prayer can fall prey to becoming a self-focused prayer time. Ironically, we want to take shortcuts with our confession time because we do not like having a magnifying glass held up to our shortcomings. We also are tempted to rush through praise and thanksgiving as well to get to the 'real' prayer time. We must avoid this temptation at all costs. (Well, maybe not compared to sinking into the sea, but *virtually* all costs.) We must not allow our prayer time to deteriorate into a series of requests to God for ourselves.

Gale Sayers, the renowned football player for the Chicago Bears, titled his autobiography *I Am Third*. He saw this phrase on a plaque on someone's desk. When he inquired about the meaning, he was given the full explanation: "God is first, others are second, I am third." He liked this concept so much he decided to adopt it as the philosophy for his own life.

This is a good prayer philosophy to adopt, to keep us from falling into self-centeredness. It just so happens that our index finger, which can work independent of the other fingers, can remind us to shift the emphasis away from ourselves. Remember that the primary purposes of our index finger are to point, show a direction, or otherwise engage in something away from us. As its emphasis is generally away from ourselves, so too should the request-based prayers have an emphasis away from ourselves. This is not meant to produce martyrs, for Christ did not neglect himself or not pray for himself. It is just that the emphasis and priority of our prayers should be on God and others, even when we are presenting requests to God.

Now with the index finger complete we have worked our way through praise, confession, thanksgiving, and intercession. We have tried to align our heart and soul with God while seeking to avoid the trap of self-centeredness in our prayer time. As we close all of our fingers, we almost make a fist. In fact, we can pick up some things by grasping at them with our four fingers, drawing objects into our palm in a rough fashion. Yet with just our four fingers, the process of grabbing objects seems crude and difficult. Anything we do grab will be held weakly, easily dropped or torn from our grasp. We are still missing something to complete a strong and useful grip with our hands. That something is our thumb.

Chapter 6

SURRENDER:
THE SOURCE OF OUR STRENGTH

*B*ehold the mighty thumb, anchor of the hand. It is the position of our thumb, opposing our fingers, that enables us to pick up and grasp items. The thumb was seen as one of the key signs of strength in the Old Testament. Part of the dedication ceremony of Hebrew priests involved placing blood on the right thumb. Canaanite King Adoni-Bezek in the Book of Judges would cut off the thumbs of captured kings to show his power over them, rendering them powerless to give any future resistance without their thumbs.

It is the thumb that provides the strength to our grip. To test this, grasp something with just your four fingers and see how easily it can be pulled loose. Then grab the same object with a full grip, including your thumb, and see how much more tightly the grip is maintained over that object. In the same way, our thumb can remind us of the source of the strength in our prayers, which is an attitude of surrender to God.

It is one thing to spend time praising God, confessing our sins, maintaining an attitude of thanksgiving, and seeking His blessing on our requests before Him. We can complete this prayer time and still maintain our personal autonomy. While we recognize that God is greater than us, we still cling to our independence. In doing so, however, we lose the source of strength in our relationship with God. Our strength comes from an attitude of surrender, where we renounce our personal autonomy and declare our dependence on God.

Not My Will, but Thy Will

The first and most crucial area where we

need to surrender is our will. This is perhaps the most difficult task for a human being to accomplish. The Original Sin in the Garden was based on an appeal to man's will; that he did not have to abide by God's command. Ever since that initial rejection of God's will, mankind has been in rebellion against God. Even redeemed humans will struggle against submitting our wills to God's divine will for our lives. Since we are not robots, we will have wills and the temptation to exercise them over surrendering to God.

Jesus modeled the proper attitude of recognizing His will and still surrendering it to God. While praying in the Garden of Gethsemane, He acknowledged that He did not desire to go through the suffering which lay ahead of Him. His human side wished to avoid the suffering if possible. Yet He fully surrendered Himself to God in saying, "Yet not as I will, but as you will," (Matt. 26:39). Jesus understood the importance of relinquishing His right to assert His own will over God's. It was this very act of surrendering His will and embracing God's will that provided Him strength in His ordeal of suffering and death.

We can realize that same strength when

we relinquish our right to self-determination in favor of surrender to God. Decision making does not have to rest on our fallible shoulders. We experience the incredible freedom from having to make our own destiny by placing our future destiny in God's hands. Yet even as we recognize the wisdom of letting God's will rule in our lives, we resist yielding control. We give in to God grudgingly, inch by inch, as we learn by experience that God truly does know better than us. This slow progress would appear comical to an all-knowing God if it were not tragic, as we struggle through a lifelong learning process of surrendering our will to God in all areas.

Here am I Lord, Send Me

Once we are on the path of surrendering our will to God, we can apply this attitude of surrender to our decision-making and actions. Isaiah demonstrated this in Isa. 6:1-8, where he works through an experience similar to the prayer time described in this book. First, Isaiah experiences the glory of God on His throne with the angels surrounding Him and worshipping

Him. Isaiah responds in despair that he is ruined, "For I am a man of unclean lips." Then an angel brings a coal to cleanse Isaiah's lips, declaring that his sin has been atoned for. Following this intense spiritual experience, God announces, "Whom shall I send? And who will go for us?" Isaiah's immediate response was, "Here am I. Send me!"

The process of knowing the glory of God, admitting his own sinfulness, and then knowing God's atoning love had brought transformation in Isaiah. He was God's servant, ready to go wherever God needed him to be. Our will is not inclined to obey God, due to residual sin nature. It takes the work of God through these stages of worship, confession, restoration, and thanksgiving to bend our wills so that they can be submitted to God's will, with obedience to God's will displayed through our words and actions.

It is important to note that Isaiah did not know where God wanted him to go or what God wanted him to say when he volunteered. All he knew was that God needed him for something, and at that stage, that was all Isaiah needed to know. How often do we evaluate things, and weigh different options, before finally making a decision. This makes sense if it is something in which we are not sure of God's will. However, when we hear God call, we need to obey Him instead of counting the cost or determining whether or not we can make a certain sacrifice. If God calls, we must answer, "Here am I. Send me!" Perhaps we do not hear God's call because we are not listening, or we drown out His still, small voice with the noise of busyness. Then again we might choose to not listen for God because we know that we would then have to obey, and we still desire to have our own will rule our life instead of submitting to God. We would do well to follow Isaiah's example, to first interact fully with God in knowing His glory and our sinfulness, and then submitting our will to God in our decisions and actions.

Surrender and the Fight with Our Sinful Nature

One of the ongoing struggles in Christian living is the battle with our will, particularly regarding trying to overcome and stamp out our sinful nature. We fight this battle, racking up both victories and defeats, as we struggle to obey God. We grimace as we hear of victorious Christian living and the ease with which habitual sins are cast aside, because our experience has been different. Our progress seems as slow and difficult as it is to swim upstream against a fast-moving river. We feel as if we are somehow losers in the Christian life, especially compared with the heroes we read about in the Bible.

Perhaps we were not reading Romans 7 closely enough, paying special attention to verses 14-25. Here Paul recounts his struggle against his sinful nature. We hear Paul's frustration as he does the things he does not want to do while being unable to do the things he desires to do. He feels as if his body is at war with itself, and finally cries out in verse 24, "Who will rescue me from this body of death?" Paul understood that his new nature in Christ was battling his old sinful nature, so the feelings of an internal war raging were accurate. We can take heart in the truth that the struggle we face as we battle our old nature over obeying God is the very struggle that Paul faced. The heroes of the Bible were not immune to the struggles against the sin nature.

In fact, we should be more concerned if we are not facing struggles of any kind. Our sinful nature is tied to our "body of death" as Paul so eloquently referred to our physical selves. We are shackled to this corrupted body on this side of eternity. The struggle comes from desiring to be a slave to God's law and in submission to him. Our sinful nature will not surrender to us without a fight. It might back off for a season and retreat sullenly to the corner, waiting for an opportunity to surprise us when we least expect it. But it does not give up. So we must be careful that a lack of struggle does not mean that we have stopped fighting our sinful nature and are letting it reign in our lives.

This concept of never-ending struggle may sound depressing, but it makes the need for surrender to God all the more important. Fighting our old nature in our own strength is extremely tiring, partially because our old nature is ready to betray us and sabotage our personal efforts. In Romans 7 Paul saw Jesus Christ as his rescuer from his body of death. Jesus can be our rescuer as well, as we surrender to Him and let Him rescue us. The battle against our old nature is very draining, and we do not have the strength to carry on the fight indefinitely. God is all-powerful, and if we allow Him to take on the fight, we can find rest in Him. This does not mean we will not be aware of the struggle, and not experience the frustration of the battle of the wills within us. It means that we have an ally and advocate ready to fight on our behalf. Our job is to step out of the way and let Him carry on the fight for us.

Whose are We, Anyway?

Paul's conclusion in Romans 7 was that while his sinful nature was a slave to sin, in his mind he was a slave to God. He carries this theme of being owned by God in other letters as well, referring to himself as a "slave of Christ," and reminding us in 1 Cor. 6:20 that "you were bought at a price." This concept of being a slave and being bought implies ownership. We as believers in the finished work of Jesus Christ belong to God.

So why is it such a struggle to continually surrender to the One who has already bought us, who has redeemed us from our bondage to sin? This is especially confusing when we know that we have the power of God at our disposal, ready to vanquish the sin nature shackled to our bodies. What makes the practice of surrender, which seems so obvious in theory, so maddeningly difficult to apply in daily living?

One possible answer is in understanding how circus elephants were once trained. When they were young and small, the elephants were tied to a large stake driven into the ground. They were convinced when they were small that the stake was too strong for them, that it was impossible to break free or tear the stake out. Once they grew up, they could easily rip out the stake if they wanted. But their lesson of weakness and impotence learned when they were young stayed with them throughout their lives. We were in the same position before accepting Christ as our Savior. We were shackled to our sinful nature, unable to break free. While Christ has broken that bondage to sin, we are continually reminded of our old nature due to being tied to our own personal "body of death." We forget that God has given us the power to overcome sin and achieve victory because of our ongoing reminder of our defeated past.

This is why a prayer of surrender is so crucial. Our strength comes from God, not our own efforts. Paul in discussing dealing with his personal thorn, concludes in 2 Cor. 12:9, 10, "Therefore I will boast all the more gladly about my weaknesses, that Christ's power may rest on me. For when I am weak, then I am strong." Paul knew that Christ was his source of power, and that this came from an ongoing surrender to God. This is the victory! Not that we can overcome our sinful nature, but that God has already overcome our sin and is ready to operate through us.

We must yield ourselves to God, then, to allow God's power to work through us. Our will must be daily and continually given over to God so that we no longer seek to rule over ourselves. This is the essence of a prayer of surrender. We can see it in the responses of Jesus at Gethsemane, in Isaiah viewing God on the throne, and in Paul battling his sinful nature as part of daily living. This attitude of surrender must be a constant decision, whether we are facing a life-changing event or the small details of our daily lives.

Since our thumb provides the strength to the grip of our hand, we can be reminded that our surrender provides God's strength to our lives and our prayers. If we remove our thumb from our grip and try to use only our fingers, we lose the strength and stability that our thumb provides to our grip. If we remove an attitude of surrender from our prayer times and assert our will, we remove God's strength and stability from our daily lives and are reduced to making it on our own. Just as it is ludicrous to try and maintain a strong grip without our thumb, our times of growth occur when we realize how ridiculous it is to try to obey God without making use of the strength God readily supplies. Once we finally catch on to the folly of our ways, we surrender that aspect of our lives and experience growth and transformation in God's likeness. This is the strength of surrender as practiced at the conclusion of our prayer times.

Chapter 7

GETTING A GRIP ON PRAYER

*T*he dictionary defines 'handy' as "readily accessible," "useful, convenient," or "easy to use or handle." Our hands fit these definitions well, because they are readily accessible, useful, convenient, and easy to use. It could even be said that our hands are downright handy! (Sorry, couldn't resist.) But seriously, our hands would be a lot less useful if they were attached anywhere besides the ends of our arms. Having our hands positioned opposite each other means that they can work together to grab, hold, and carry items too large for one hand. Our hands really are the epitome of 'handy,' and likely the source of that term.

Before this deteriorates any further down the track of shamelessly bad hand puns, consider how God designed our hands. Their brilliant structure, with four fingers and an opposable thumb, and their position both on our bodies and in conjunction to each other, allows us to do an almost limitless variety of tasks related to daily living. Our hands work well together, individually, and as individual fingers, and truly are an integral part of our lives.

Prayer should also be an integral part of our lives. But too often prayer is reserved for special times and places such as before dinner, at church, and in case of an emergency. We do not pull our hands out only when needed or leave them home if they are not needed; they go with us wherever we are and are a part of virtually everything we do. The same should be true with prayer. It should not be something pulled out on certain occasions, but rather we should "pray continually" (1 Thess. 5:17). The attitude of "ready to pray" should be with us wherever we go and part of whatever we do.

Putting it all Together

Hopefully this pattern of using the fingers on your hand to balance your prayer life can help prayer become more natural and continual in your life. The goal for prayer is to not be like a tool pulled out of a box when needed but to be like a part of your body, with you wherever you go. God is with us wherever we are, although there may be times that we, like Adam, might wish to hide from God. Since we know that hiding from or running from God is not possible (see Adam and Jonah), we should embrace the opportunity to enter into fellowship with God at any time through prayer.

Back when printed telephone books were common (before the Internet), there was an advertisement encouraging customers to "let your fingers do the walking through the Yellow Pages." The point of the commercial was that the Yellow Pages portion of the telephone book organized businesses by type, making it easier to find what was needed. Through your fingers walking through the book and finding the correct business, valuable time would be saved by calling rather than driving around town finding the right business. In the same way, this pattern of each finger representing a different element of prayer organizes our prayer lives and saves us the trouble of trying to think of how to pray or how we should connect with God.

God is multi-faceted, with a personality and character too rich and complex for us to begin to comprehend. By introducing these five components into our regular prayer life, we can experience more of the richness of God's personality than we could by focusing on one or two types of prayer. While we can never experience all the richness of God, it is desirable to know Him as completely as possible, which involves coming to God in a variety of ways. This balanced prayer pattern provides five different types or attitudes of prayer within one prayer time.

Letting Our Hand Work Naturally – as a Team

The best prayer life is a balanced prayer life. If our prayer consisted entirely of petitioning God, we would begin to perceive God as an eternal Santa Claus, bestowing gifts upon us to satisfy our whims. On the other hand, if our prayer consisted entirely of praise and confession, we might see God as either too far above us or ourselves as too low below God to build an intimate relationship with Him. Imagine a relationship with someone that had just one item or topic as the primary or even sole focus of that relationship. Because of the one-dimensional nature, the relationship would lack depth and quickly grow stale. We need all these components of prayer to build the proper healthy relationship with God.

Just as God is complex, a quick look at creation demonstrates that He is also a God of limitless variety. Therefore, there is no need to use this pattern the exact same way every time you pray. Listening to people drone through the Lord's Prayer will show that any pattern, regardless of how inspired, can become a routine and a rut rather than a vibrant time with God. To avoid this pattern becoming another routine, try variations on the straight praise-confession-thanksgiving-intercession-surrender pattern. While it is normally good to start with praise, the

Hebrews generally began their Lament Psalms with a complaint, because that was their attitude at that point, and God desires honesty. Once they began voicing their honest feelings to God, and remembered who God is and His love for them in the midst of their difficulties, they could move into praise and continue in other types of prayer from that point.

Another helpful variation I have used is to praise God about one topic, then confess my failure and sin regarding that topic, and then thank God for His provision and care regarding that same topic. I then repeat the praise-confession-thanksgiving triad through multiple topics. That may be all that is needed at that point, although it is also good to generally end a prayer time with an attitude of surrender to God, because the point of surrender is to remind us to place ourselves under God's will and care.

While variation helps to avoid repetition, keep in mind the way the hand is designed. Although only two or three fingers are needed to pick up or hold something, the grip is weaker. The strongest grip involves the entire hand, with all of the fingers and thumb engaged. In the same way, this prayer pattern is most effective when engaging all five components on a regular basis. The goal is to have overall balance in your prayer life in the long term, even while praying only some of the components at some times. So if you find yourself falling into a pattern of emphasizing a couple of the components and neglecting others, you should return to using all five elements in prayer to restore that balance to your prayer life. Hopefully, the balance of your fingers within your hand can remind you that just as each finger can stand on its own, the hand is most effective when all five fingers are engaged regularly. The same is true in our prayer lives: not all components of prayer will be used all the time, but they should all be used regularly and consistently.

Letting Our Hand Work Naturally – as Individual Units

While this pattern is designed to work together to achieve a balanced and more effective prayer life, it is not necessary to insist on praying all five components every time you connect with God. The reality is that we will have established times to focus on God, but that we will not always be in a place where we can stop what we are doing for an engaged prayer time. Many of our prayers will be on the run and in response to a sudden situation. God understands our lives and hearts as we move through the urgency of life.

So do not fret if an instinctive response is to petition God in a moment of crisis. Do not feel guilt for blurting out a need without preceding it with praise, confession, and thanksgiving. When Nehemiah was asked by the king what he wanted concerning the situation in Jerusalem, he quickly prayed before answering the king. The words of Nehemiah's prayer in Neh. 2:4 are not recorded, and it was likely a quick, silent prayer that did not incorporate formal times of praise, confession, thanksgiving, and surrender. What is recorded, however, is Nehemiah's prayer in Nehemiah 1, which shows his praise, confession, thanksgiving, and surrender over a period of three months. Because Nehemiah spent extended time in prayer, balancing these components in prayer to God, his heart was where it needed to be when quick supplication was needed.

There may be times when we simply need

to pour out our hearts before God, recognizing our sinfulness and pleading for His mercy. This was the focus of the prayers in Nehemiah 9 and Ezra 9, times of national confession felt by the individuals. There may be other times when our focus is on praise and thanksgiving. Many praise services are structured in this manner where the emphasis is on God's goodness and His great deeds of love, both past and present. Each component can stand on its own in addition to being part of a pattern. This is not meant to diminish the importance of using the pattern as a whole as mentioned above, but seeks to provide examples of variations in using this pattern to achieve a balanced and effective prayer life.

If You want to Grow in Prayer, Raise Your Hand

The prayer pattern as a whole is part of the ongoing preparation for and work in building our relationship with God. We use it in times when we can focus on God, and build the pattern into our lives. Then, in times of crisis, the pattern is already built into us to rely upon when we are in need. After Wellington defeated Napoleon, he stated, "The battle of Waterloo was won on the playing fields of Eton." His point was that the preparation and training done at Eton school, even during times of apparent play, gave his army what was needed to prevail when the test came during the battle. God uses our prayer lives to both enjoy present fellowship together and to develop us for future times of service.

We cannot prepare for a crisis when the crisis arrives; all our preparation comes prior to the crisis. Since it is difficult to know when a crisis will occur, preparation must be done as a part of daily living. So if we want to turn to God first during a crisis, we must practice turning to God first during our routine days. Thomas á Kempis states, "One habit overcomes another." The time to develop the new habit of turning to God, of being continually reminded by our hands that God is with us, is during times of relative calm. A person will instinctively turn to what they know when they are under pressure. We must practice turning to God daily during calm times so that when the pressure mounts, we naturally turn to God.

That is the key to using your hand as a prompt to prayer. Since it is with you all the time, it becomes a constant reminder to turn to God. Because each finger represents a different component of prayer, our hand reminds us of the different ways in which we should approach God. Think back to your initial prayer of salvation. You acknowledged God as good and holy, confessed that you were a sinner, admitted that you could do nothing to either bring yourself into relationship with God or pay for your sins, and asked for Jesus to be your Savior and Lord, thanking Him for His work on the Cross. That simple prayer of salvation contained these five elements of prayer. Because these are foundational components of our Christian life, they are easy to remember, understand, and take with us wherever we go. Our hand just becomes an easy reminder to reach out to God throughout our days. Our fingers and thumb aid that reminder by spurring us on to a varied and balanced prayer life when reaching up to God.

Chapter 8

LETTING GOD GET A GRIP ON YOU

*T*ake another look at the palm of your hand. Notice the lines, both large and small, that form on the surface whenever you bend or fold your hand. Look to see if your fingers are either long and slender or shorter and more solid. Closely examine your fingerprints and thumbprint, which are understood to be unique. While other people may have similar patterns, no one else on earth has the exact matching fingerprint. This simple fact highlights the truth that while all of us were designed in a generally similar fashion, God has made each of us uniquely in His image.

Now look at the features on your hand that have been added after birth. You may have calluses or scars, or even have shifted your fingers through your activities in life. Back when more people worked with their hands and fewer worked in offices, it was said that you could determine a person's occupation through a close look at their hands.

On one hand (har!), we have the hands that God gave us at birth, with a unique combination of size and strength and fingerprints. Since then our hands have been molded and shaped by our experiences in life. Our hands as we view them today reflect both their initial state and our lifetime of using them.

In the same way, we have all been given the same salvation through the shed blood of Jesus Christ, and have all received the same indwelling Spirit. But then we have all been uniquely gifted by the Spirit to glorify God and build up the body of Christ. We have been given individual talents and lived unique experiences so that our spiritual experience is unique. We have also made choices about what we do with what God has given us, and how we allow God to shape and mold us. Our prayer lives will reflect both our initial salvation in Christ and our spiritual experience after that decision.

The Heart of Prayer

Children have the most exquisite little hands, with their fingers and thumb so tiny and yet perfectly formed. They easily fit inside larger adult hands, swallowed up entirely within the adult's palm. At that point the child is dependent on the adult, secure in the comfort and protection of the bigger, stronger person in whom they have placed their hand. Even as we continue to grow up and age, holding hands is an intimate act displaying both comfort and security.

It is this same combination of dependence, security, intimacy, and comfort which lies at the heart of our prayer times with God. Just as we recognize that our hands are unique while following a standard pattern, our relationship with God will be unique while displaying common characteristics. We can grow in intimacy with God through prayer. We can receive comfort from God in prayer. We can rest in the security of God's love in prayer. Finally, we can declare our dependence on God through prayer. While the rest of the world keeps asserting its autonomy, we use prayer to return to God, trusting in Him, secure in Him, dependent on Him.

We have to remember, though, that prayer is not about us. It is about us reaching out to God. We must make sure that as we reach out to God, it is in fellowship and dependence rather than selfish motives. Our task during prayer is to turn our thoughts and desires from ourselves to God. Our heart in the old nature is willful and stubborn, always looking out for our selfish ends. The heart of prayer is to make the attitude adjustment where our heart becomes aligned with God's heart, and we begin to see things through His eyes.

The Goal of Prayer

Notice that so much of following God is simply obeying God rather than doing great things for Him. King Saul was rejected by God for disobedience in 1 Samuel 15, because Saul brought back livestock instead of totally destroying a nearby people. When Saul protested that he brought back the livestock as a sacrifice to God, he received this reply, "Does the Lord delight in burnt offerings and sacrifices as much as in obeying the voice of the Lord?" (1 Sam. 15:22). God does not desire us to achieve great things for Him so much as He desires that we obey Him.

The easiest way to obey God is to have our heart and will aligned with Him. Saul failed in this regard because he was choosing his own will over God's. So when we assert our own will, we disobey God. When we follow what God wants, submitting to His will, we obey God.

So how do we know what God wants in any given situation? The Bible gives some specific answers, but it seems to give more principles than specifics. The answer can be seen in two Old Testament men, Enoch and Moses. We are told that "Enoch walked with God" (Gen. 5:22) and that God "would speak with Moses face to face, as a man speaks with his friend" (Ex. 33:11). These men had continual fellowship with God, so constant that Enoch was said to be walking with God. Paul echoed this concept when he encouraged the Thessalonians to "Pray continually" (1 Thess. 5:17). Prayer is the best means of establishing continual fellowship with God, to be "walking with God."

What are we trying to accomplish when we pray? The answer is found in understanding the heart of prayer. If our heart is askew and not aligned with God, then our goals will be off target and our whole purpose suspect. A good definition of the purpose of prayer comes from Emilie Griffin, who said, "Prayer is neither to impress other people nor to impress God. It's not to be taken on with a mentality of success. The goal, in prayer, is to give oneself away."

To whom or what are we to give ourselves away then? The answer is very simple: whose are we? To whom do we belong? If we belong to God, then through prayer we are giving ourselves to God. We can have the same attitude as Isaiah, who declared, "Here am I. Send me!" We can be ready for whatever God wants for us. Obedience becomes easier because we have dealt with our heart and attitude problems in prayer. We use prayer so that we, too, can walk with God.

The Result of Prayer

What happens when we pray? What difference does prayer make? There are simply too many accounts of prayer being effective, both in the Bible and the history of the Church, to recount here. Peter's miraculous escape from prison in Acts 12 and the events surrounding Saul's conversion in Acts 9 are but two examples of effective prayer. Churches and families have reconciled, coming back from the brink of splitting up. There are entire books testifying to the vast miraculous works of God, all apparently fueled by prayer.

Yet there are times when, from a human perspective, prayer did not work or change things. A cursory reading of Foxe's *Book of Martyrs* shows that many Christians died, often gruesomely, despite prayers for deliverance. It is tempting to think that answers to prayer are random or arbitrary, or worse, a capricious God granting or withholding His favor on a whim.

Those temptations must be cast aside in favor of an honest look at the God of the Bible. As we learned in our time of praise and thanksgiving, God has many good and great attributes, including love, compassion, patience, and constancy. God is faithful and keeps His promises. Yet God is also sovereign, and his ways are not our ways, so it will be impossible to understand all decisions on this side of eternity. It is at those times that we must cling to the good attributes we do know, just as the ancient Israelites did when they wrote the Lament Psalms. Despite whatever misfortune befell them, they trusted in God's goodness.

So we know that prayer can have an impact on events, but we also know that God is sovereign. The one constant result of prayer, regardless of any external changes, is the internal change occurring in our hearts. As we submit ourselves to God, as we recognize God for who He is and what He has done, we allow God to transform our hearts. Then we can be in alignment with God and it becomes easier to walk with God in obedience. This is the result of prayer.

God's People of Prayer

God desires prayer. Both Solomon and Jesus referred to the Temple as "a house of prayer." Notice that the emphasis was not a house of sacrifice or a house of worship, but of prayer. God's people are identified through their prayer relationship with God. 2 Chron. 7:14 illustrates this dynamic of being a people of prayer and the life God blesses:

> *If my people* – we belong to God;
> *who are called by my name* – we are
> known as God's people;
> *will humble themselves* – we
> must stop fighting God and
> asserting ourselves,
> *and pray* – prayer is always at the
> center of our relationship with
> God,
> *and seek my face* - we must seek
> God and draw close to Him,
> *and turn from their wicked ways* – we
> must repent;
> *THEN*
> *I will hear from heaven* – God hears
> the prayers of those turning to
> Him,
> *and will forgive* – God is ready to
> receive us back into fellowship,
> *and will heal their land* – God is
> ready to bestow blessings upon
> His people.

Prayer is the central activity that gets God's attention and restores us to fellowship with Him. Prayer is what turns us around from going in the wrong direction to walking with God. Prayer strengthens our relationship with God to experience His blessings.

The church in Acts was a praying church, as seen in various miraculous escapes and healings that occurred. But their prayer was not just during a crisis, it was part of their regular life. This pattern continued throughout the early church period, which caused it to grow tremendously despite opposition from both Jewish and Roman authorities.

Today we have the resources, lack of persecution, and skills to see tremendous growth in the church, yet we seem to be moving rapidly yet not progressing. Studies show that many current youth and young adults have rejected and abandoned their parents' faith. Why is the present-day church struggling when it appears to have so much more going for it compared to the early church?

The answer seems to lie in a general lack of prayer among the church. We are so busy doing

Christian activities that we neglect the most important activity: spending time with God. As Samuel Chadwick said, "The one concern of the Devil is to keep Christians from praying. He fears nothing from prayerless religion. He laughs at our toil, mocks at our wisdom, but trembles when we pray." We must not let our efforts to serve God interfere with our need to submit to God. To follow the example of Isaiah, surrender comes first, then service. We take our marching orders from God and then move where God wants us to go; we do not take off and hope to God we are running in the right direction.

Take a final look at your hand. As you open and close it, recognize that anything you grasp is securely in your grip as you engage all of your fingers and thumb. Think of your prayer life, and how your fingers and thumb are a reminder to balance your prayer life with an emphasis of focusing on God and surrendering to God. Also remember how just as your hands are at your side wherever you go, God is dwelling within you and is with you wherever you go. God is ready to be in fellowship with you, your job is to remember that God *is* with you at all times and you are not limited to relying on your own strength. Finally, think about the grip your hand builds as you close your fingers and thumb, and how this pattern can help you get a better grip on your prayer life. Now turn it around, and understand that through the process of surrender and conforming to God's image, when you thought you were getting a better grip on your prayer life you were actually allowing God to get a better grip on you. Through your stronger prayer life, you can go through your days as God's person, safe and secure in the palm of God's hand.

REVIEW QUESTIONS

*T*he following pages provide review questions for each chapter. They will both review the information given as well as prompt further thoughts. These questions can be used as a self-study or in a group setting.

One recommendation in both individual and group settings is to read the referenced passages as a group to understand the context. While an explanation of the context was given and the effort made to not take the interpretation of the verses out of their proper contexts, reading the passage provides a fuller understanding of the setting for that prayer or event.

It is my hope that this review can help further ingrain the concepts discussed in this book to aid you in strengthening your prayer life. While building our prayer lives is a worthy goal, it should not be our final goal. Prayer is the means by which we connect to God, with our ultimate goal of being transformed, of being conformed into His image. That is my prayer for you.

Chapter 1
A Hand-y Guide to Effective Prayer
Review Questions

1. How would you describe your prayer life at the present time: growing, stagnant, or withering on the vine?

2. Review these prayer diagnosis questions: Is your prayer time working in unison with God or out of joint and trying to impose your will upon God? Are you enjoying a variety of prayer types and styles, or has it deteriorated into bland sameness? Is your emphasis on God or yourself when you do pray? Determine the relative healthiness of your prayer life.

3. When faced with a crisis, do you instinctively turn toward God or look to figure out the problem on your own?

4. Do you meet with God on a regular basis, or is your time with Him more random and sporadic?

5. How aware are you of God's presence as you go through your normal day?
6. Take time to examine your hand, and then fold your hands and pray, seeking God's guidance and support as you begin a new plan of building your prayer life.

CHAPTER 2
PRAISE:
WHAT APPEARS LITTLE IS ACTUALLY BIG
REVIEW QUESTIONS

1. What are the primary purposes of praising God in our prayer times?
2. Look at the beginning of Psalms 29, 34, 48, 92, 117, and 135. What do these passages say about praising God? What do they say about us in relation to God?
3. What character qualities of God can you name? Why are these attributes worthy of praise?
4. What does God declare about Himself in Ex. 34:6?
5. Reflect on the names of God as listed in Isa. 9:6. What do they mean, and why are they worthy of praise?
6. Select one of the names of God "Jehovah-" from the list. Read the context of the name and take the time to understand how God is working in the

same manner in your life today. Take time to praise God for His character qualities being evident both past and present.

CHAPTER 3
CONFESSION:
THE LOGICAL SECOND STEP IN PRAYER
REVIEW QUESTIONS

1. One of the biggest problems in confessing sin is honestly examining ourselves. How hard is it for you to admit when you have done something wrong? Do you accept responsibility for your actions, or do you find excuses and try to blame other people and circumstances?

2. Before you begin the process of confession, decide if you really want to turn to God. Do you really want to stop what you are doing?

3. Do you accept God's grace in your life, or do you continue to punish yourself over sins committed? Do you ever feel that what you have done is too bad for God to forgive? These thoughts are wrong and need to be rejected.

4. Read the parable of the unmerciful servant (Matt. 18:23-35). Have you been able to forgive those who have wronged you? Take the time to begin this process before bitterness takes root.

5. Take time to personally work through the process of confession, repentance, and restoration with God. While uncomfortable and even painful, the resultant cleansing will leave you freer and able to draw closer to God.

CHAPTER 4
THANKSGIVING:
RESPONSE TO GOD'S WORK IN OUR LIVES
REVIEW QUESTIONS

1. What is the distinction between praise and thanksgiving?

2. Read Psalm 136. What events and actions are recorded here? How is God's character displayed in His actions?

3. Remember back to the time of salvation. What specific events or people were involved in the process of bringing you to salvation? Take time to thank God for your salvation, including the specific activities leading you to that point.

4. Take time to look at your past week. What seemingly little things can actually be seen as God's general and ongoing grace in your life? Take time to thank God for the little daily good things in your life.

5. Think of a difficult situation or trial in

your life. Can you thank God in advance for how He will act, without knowing when or how God will act?

6. Read and meditate on Psalm 100. Are there parallels between the events in that Psalm and what has happened in your own life? For example, do you feel that you are God's and one of His sheep to be cared for in His pasture? Praise and thank God for what He is doing in your life that is similar to what is described in this Psalm.

7. In the same manner that the Israelites built a stone memorial to remember to be thankful to God for His deliverance and protection, is there some item in your life that you can use as a memorial to remind you to be thankful for God's work in your life?

CHAPTER 5
INTERCESSION: OUR REQUESTS BEFORE GOD
REVIEW QUESTIONS

1. What is the distinction between intercession and supplication in making prayer requests to God?
2. On what basis do we bring requests to God? What is our hope in presenting requests to God?
3. What is the importance of not beginning our prayer time with intercession, but instead preceding intercession with praise, confession, and thanksgiving?
4. How should we pray when we do not know the right request to pray?
5. How can we emphasize others in our prayer time and yet not neglect ourselves? What example of intercessory praying did Jesus provide in John 17?

Chapter 6
Surrender: The Source of Our Strength
Review Questions

1. The battle over surrender to God involves what aspect of our person? How did Jesus achieve victory here in Matt. 26:39?

2. In Isaiah 6, how did Isaiah demonstrate surrender to God?

3. In Rom. 7:14-25, how does Paul describe the battle occurring within him. In who or what is his hope of victory?

4. What is our goal when we pray a prayer of surrender to God?

5. How does the act of surrendering to God make our prayer lives stronger?

CHAPTER 7
GETTING A GRIP ON PRAYER
REVIEW QUESTIONS

1. How does using our hand to remind us of five components of prayer help to achieve a more balanced prayer life?

2. Is it critical to pray all five types of prayer every time we pray?

3. When can a prayer pattern become a routine or rut? How do we work against this happening?

4. How can building our prayer lives when things are going well help prepare us to manage times of crisis?

5. How can our hand aid in building our prayer lives?

CHAPTER 8
LETTING GOD GET A GRIP ON YOU
REVIEW QUESTIONS

1. How are some ways you are similar to your family? Are there any distinctive similarities compared to other people? How are you unique, even among your family and especially compared to other people?

2. How has God uniquely shaped you, through your gifts, talents, personality, and experiences?

3. How can you better focus your prayer life on God and not on yourself?

4. What is the purpose of prayer?

5. What happens, both around you and inside you, when you pray?

6. How can you let your prayer life be a means to let God get a better grip on you?